LEVEL 2 READER

SURPRISING SWIMMERS

By Emma Ryan

SCHOLASTIC INC.

Photos ©: cover splashy text and splash art and throughout: Semiletava Hanna/Shutterstock; cover wave art and throughout: Big_Ryan and enjoynz/Getty Images; cover main: Steve Bloom Images/Stevebloom.com; back cover: Richard Peterson/Shutterstock; 1: Richard Peterson/Shutterstock; 2-3 main: tristan tan/Shutterstock; 3 background: Anna segeren/Shutterstock; 4 header background and throughout: aleksandarvelasevic/Getty Images; 4 main: DenGuy/Getty Images; 5: Jane Burton/Minden Pictures; 6-7 main: MarclSchauer/Shutterstock; 7 inset: BMCL/Shutterstock; 8 background speckle and throughout: barbaliss/Shutterstock; 8 left: Joao Virissimo/Shutterstock; 8 right: Richard Peterson/Shutterstock; 8-9 main: creatives/Getty Images; 10 inset: Johan Swanepoel/Shutterstock; 10-11 main: Johnny Haglund/Getty Images; 12-13 main: Henrik Winther Andersen/Shutterstock; 13 inset: Iakov Filimonov/Shutterstock; 14 inset: Eric Isselée/Shutterstock; 14-15 main: cynoclub/Shutterstock; 16: Mike Tan/Shutterstock; 17: Hannamariah/Shutterstock; 19: tswinner/Getty Images; 20-21 main: Kirsten Wahlquist/Shutterstock; 20 inset: Jane Vargas/Seapics.com; 22-23 main: GelatoPlus/Getty Images; 23 inset: Leksele/Shutterstock; 24: jtylerbrown/Getty Images; 25: ElsvanderGun/Getty Images; 26: Ilias Strachinis/Shutterstock; 27: Riegsecker/Getty Images; 28-29 main: Patrick Rolands/Shutterstock; 29 inset: Anan Kaewkhammul/Shutterstock; 30: Marilyn Nieves/Getty Images; 31: tororo reaction/Shutterstock.

ISBN 978-0-545-55266-0

18 19 20 21 22 23 24 25 26 27   40   28 27 26 25 24 23 22 21 20 19

Printed in the U.S.A.
First printing, January 2013
Book design by Kay Petronio

Forget fish—have you ever seen an elephant swim? Did you know that lots of other animals can swim too, like pigs and tigers? Want to find out more? Dive in to see which creatures go wild for water!

CAT

Though many cats can swim, most don't like getting wet. Even giving a cat a bath can be a challenge for pet owners.

However, the Turkish Van, also known as the swimming cat, doesn't mind at all.

TURKISH VAN

CATS ARE MAMMALS.

TIGER

Even though most **domestic** cats don't like the water, the largest cat in the world is a good swimmer! Tigers can usually be found living near water.

TIGERS CAN WEIGH UP TO 500 POUNDS.

They'll take a dip to cool off when it's hot outside.

PIG

You've probably heard of the doggie paddle, but what about the piggy paddle? Not only do pigs swim, but there's even a place nicknamed Pig Island in the Bahamas where visitors can pay to swim with them!

The Bahamas are a group of islands located in the Caribbean Sea.

NASSAU

ELEPHANT

You might be surprised to learn that elephants are excellent swimmers! They actually use their long trunk

as a **snorkel** for breathing. They also use their trunk to suck up water and spray it on themselves to cool off.

11

POLAR BEAR

You've probably seen polar bears swimming at a zoo, but do you know why they're so good at it? They have webbed feet, similar to a duck's feet, which help them paddle through the water.

Sometimes polar bears travel by water and can swim for hours at a time without stopping.

HORSE

Other animals and humans also use water therapy for pain or injuries.

It's definitely unusual to see a horse swimming, but water is a common treatment for injured horses. Especially for ones that race! Exercising in giant pools can help horses with pain.

DOG

Did you know that not all dogs can swim? Some **breeds** are better at it than others. Labrador Retrievers and Golden Retrievers are good swimmers because of their strong legs. Bulldogs and Dachshunds have short legs, making it hard for them to stay afloat.

SEA SNAKE

Sea snakes are natural-born swimmers. Their tail helps them travel easily in water. Unlike fish, snakes do not have **gills**, so they have to come up regularly for air to breathe.

SNAKES ARE REPTILES.

SEA OTTER

When they're not hunting
or swimming, these
talented mammals can
eat and sleep while
floating on their back.

PENGUIN

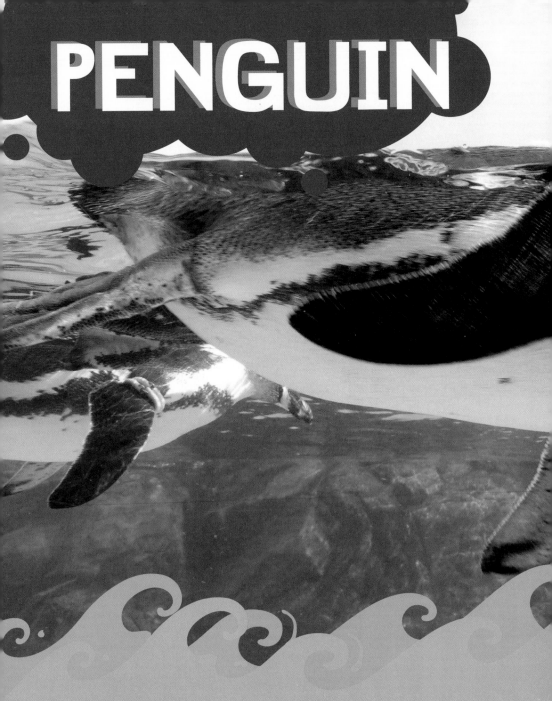

Penguins are birds that can't fly, but they can definitely swim! Their wings are used like flippers, and

Most penguins find food while swimming underwater.

their feathers help keep them warm in cold water.

SNOW MONKEY

Snow monkeys like to live in big groups and spend time on the ground and in trees. What else do they like? Swimming! The snow monkey exhibit at the Central Park Zoo in New York City has a hot tub and a pond.

AMERICAN BULLFROG

Bullfrogs are a type of frog with strong back legs and webbed feet that are perfect for swimming! Bullfrogs are usually green and have splotches on their back legs.

FROGS ARE AMPHIBIANS.

HIPPO

Hippos spend most of their lives in and around water that's not too deep. Their eyes, ears, and nostrils are located on

top of their head, so they can
see, hear, and breathe while their
body stays cool underwater.

To see even
more swimming
creatures, visit
your local zoo
or **aquarium**.

Animals that can swim go in the water for different reasons. Some animals are looking for food, some are traveling, and some just want to cool off. Others take a dip for fun—just like humans!

GLOSSARY

Amphibian: a cold-blooded animal that lives in water and breathes with gills when young

Aquarium: a place for visitors to see different kinds of ocean creatures

Breed: a particular type of plant or animal

Domestic: animals that have been tamed

Gills: a pair of organs near a fish's mouth through which it breathes by getting oxygen from water

Mammal: a warm-blooded animal that has hair or fur and usually gives birth to live babies

Reptile: a cold-blooded animal that moves across the ground or crawls on short legs

Snorkel: a long tube that you hold in your mouth and use to breathe while swimming underwater